Grip Life

Grip Life

❖

ELIZABETH W. GRUBBS

Rev. date: 03/11/2021

To order additional copies of this book, contact:
Xlibris
844-714-8691
www.Xlibris.com
Orders@Xlibris.com
826407

This book is dedicated to all humanity. It is my desire that my two sons, Osaygefo and Norman, and readers will check these seven elements of their lives periodically.

Life is a major event that involves one's past, present, and future. In each of these phases of life, there are conditions and actions that may change or alter like the weather. Life is like seasons. Its temperatures register hot, warm, cool, and cold. Life offers choices that should be decided with reasons. It is experienced in many different elements of the past and present that influence one's future. Regardless of its quality, every breathing human being participates in life daily.

—Dr. Elizabeth W. Grubbs

CONTENTS

ACKNOWLEDGMENTS

I am appreciative to Vanessa Johnson and Christine Wheeler of Brundidge, Alabama, and Sabrina Thomas, Tamika Teague, and Marion Ivey of Troy, Alabama, for encouraging me to write a book.

Well, during the COVID-19 pandemic, camped in my home, I thought a lot about life. Therefore, I began to write a book titled *Grip Life.* Having revealed this ten-year, procrastinated plan of mine to a Huntsville, Alabama, friend, he said, "Just do it!"

In addition to the above persons, I thank Felicia Darby of Luverne, Alabama, for calling me every morning for verification of my life in my body and mind!

INTRODUCTION

The purpose of this book is to inspire the reader to examine self in each of the areas of health of life and to improve in his or her lowest area and/or help someone to acquire a *grip* on life. The seven elements of life discussed in this book are physical, mental, family, financial, vocational, social, and spiritual health.

Of course, the writer's observations, interactions, and experiences, like everyone's encounters, are limited by her heritage, environment, choices, health, association, and role models in life.

Regardless of the quality of life, if one is breathing, that someone has had a past, is experiencing a present, and should be considering a future. As one embarks on the journey of life, traveling through time, that human being needs to study, change, improve, create, and maintain all or part of his or her elements of life: physical movement, thoughts, family contact, vocational responsibility, financial obligation, social interaction, and spiritual belief.

Grip Life

1. Shape your body!
2. Contact your family!
3. Pay your bills!
4. Worship your God!

5. Tune your mind!
6. Work your job!
7. Attend a social!

This book encourages one to take a serious look at self through these seven elements of life.

CHAPTER 1

Physical Health Element

Born in a small, southern town in Alabama to a married couple, and the third child of four daughters, physically I sustained my slot when dealing with siblings. Also, playing, working, and walking outdoors helped me maintain my physical fitness. Besides physical education at school, outdoor activities during my early years involved planting and harvesting mile-long rows of crops and rounding up cattle. I credit these physical activities as exercises to help me commune in nature and indirectly maintain physical fitness while completing my chores with my father. From these experiences, I learned that nature calms one's spirit, and movement is important to one's body weight and figure.

Later, I learned that Harvard Medical School representatives and American College of Sports and Medicine (ACSM), according to Laura Williams's April 3, 2020, report, revealed that physical fitness for life components should include cardiovascular endurance training, muscular strength training, and flexibility training. Therefore, I suggest that every able body should participate in some type of workout plan, whether as outdoor physical labor, indoor physical fitness, or in an adequate workout facility—individually or in a group. After all, the Centers for Disease Control (CDC) links regular physical activity to not only reducing risk of heart disease but also type 2 diabetes and some cancers, and it enhances one's mental health and therefore results in an improved quality of life.

Thus, I would advise readers of all ages to check with a doctor or other medical professional before participating in moderate or rigorous exercises. What will your Fitbit show about your movement? Nevertheless, plan to move your body, with or without a trainer, for one hour each day. In addition to physical activity, one should highly consider diet and nutrition, as they play equally important roles in one's physical health.

Adequate diet and nutrition will differ among every person and should be tailored based on circumstances surrounding one's culture, health, and overall lifestyle. Therefore, I encourage every reader to eat healthy and make good decisions about weight and exercise.

Biblical Physical Health Thought

Beloved, I pray all may go well with you and that you may be in good health, as it goes well with your soul. (3 John 1:2 ESV)

Comment

The Lord wants us to be in good health.

Your Physical Health Plan

List your physical health/fitness goals below.

_____

_____

_____

_____

_____

CHAPTER 2

Mental Health Element

Now that you are more aware of your physical health, let us focus on your mental health. Mental health is important because it is more than the absence of mental illness.

I learned mental health is valuable from a situation that occurred while I was a preteen visiting my grandmother on a nice, sunny day. I fearfully and quickly learned, in less than two hours, from a firsthand experience of witnessing actions of her neighbor who lived a half mile from her and dropped by for an unexpected visit. As the truth goes, I was keeping my grandmother company in the kitchen and setting the table for the two of us as my grandmother was cooking country ham, buttermilk pancakes, and scrambled eggs for our anticipated, delicious breakfast, when I saw Ms. Mae through the kitchen window. I informed my grandmother that Ms. Mae was walking up on her back porch.

She responded, "Let her in."

I hurried to open the door as I spoke to Ms. Mae, a strangely dressed woman still in her apron-covered nightgown and house shoes with long, unattended hair draping her shoulders. She swiftly entered and answered my good morning with "Move out of my way!" That I did as I followed her back into the kitchen.

My grandmother told me to set another table setting and told Ms. Mae to have a seat in the same breath. Looking like a forty-year-old rag doll, Ms. Mae did not sit but walked up to my grandmother at the stove, grabbed the butcher knife that my grandmother had used to slice the country ham, and placed it under my grandmother's throat. I screamed as my grandmother told Ms. Mae to sit and eat now, and in the same sentence told me to go home.

I answered immediately, "After I eat breakfast."

Ms. Mae did not sit but bit a pancake from the stove as she held the knife under my grandmother's chin. I moved to go out of the kitchen to run to get help since Ms. Mae was twice my grandmother's size, but Ms. Mae told me to sit. I sat. She moved the large knife to my grandmother's back.

My grandmother asked her if she had taken her medicine. Ms. Mae told her to walk as she put her other hand on the back of my grandmother's neck and continued to hold the knife to my granny's back. I was afraid to move. She then said to my grandmother, "Let's go!" My granny obeyed her as she said, "Out the door." My granny winked at me as they left out the back door.

I tiptoed to the front door and ran down the road a half mile in the other direction. I arrived early morning, out of breath, and beat on my dad's door. He answered the door and I told him what had happened at his mother's house. He grabbed his truck key and told me to get in his red truck.

We went by my grandmother's wide-open house, and nobody was there. He said, "Come on," as he locked the front door and I grabbed a piece of ham.

We got back into the truck, blew the horn to wake up my grandmother's neighbor, and told her to call the cops and have them meet him at Ms. Mae's house. Once there, he told me to remain in his truck.

He eased on the side of Ms. Mae's house to peep through a window. By that time, two policemen had arrived. He told them that Ms. Mae was holding a knife on his mother as his mother swept her house floor. Ms. Mae's back door was opened so they eased in after my dad explained that Ms. Mae had been in and out of the "crazy house" from time to time.

The next thing I knew, my dad had his arms around my crying grandmother as he put her into the truck with me. The cops had Ms. Mae handcuffed as the emergency wagon pulled up. My dad and I got my grandmother to calm down in her house, and she told me to warm the food. I stayed with my grandmother for the rest of the day.

Ms. Mae was admitted, long term, to an out-of-town mental health facility. I remained in this small town where I was born, until I went off to college at Tuskegee University and other institutions of higher learning. During that time, Ms. Mae never returned.

The incident got me thinking and praying, "Lord, keep me in my right mind," and later led me to researching careers related to mental health. Having been a counselor who performed case studies at a VA hospital, I realized that the mind truly is a terrible part of the body to malfunction. Thus, my definition for mental health has grown to include not just the absence of a mental illness but having the mind to perform all daily social, financial, physical, spiritual, and vocational duties; solve one's life issues; make wholesome decisions and choices about daily living operations; or seek resources of professionals to coach one through these life elements.

Have you ever thought about your mental health being a necessity to maintaining a normal life? After all, the American Psychiatric Association (APA) revealed that persons with mental disorders are characterized by patterns of abnormal behaviors that lead to impairment in everyday living to cope with life's ups and downs. If you have a friend or family member who malfunctions every week in one or more of the health elements, his or her pattern of behavior is not normal for societal interaction. Encourage the person to allow you to help him or her seek professional help to adjust the condition to acceptable society standards. This is very important to keep ill will from overtaking the person as he or she becomes worse. After all, I have not seen anyone the cops have had to discipline on the street wearing a T-shirt with the words "I am insane."

Help yourself and loved ones to keep a grip on life by seeking the proper resources by calling mental health professionals, researching through the computer, or reaching out to primary care doctors or health insurance networks for recommendations.

Keep a grip on life by being physically and mentally fit.

Biblical Mental Health Thought

Cast all your anxiety on him because he cares for you. (1 Peter 5:7 NIV)

Comment

This verse reminds us that we can pray for God to guide us to the right resources—such as the ones I've suggested—for help.

Your Mental Health Self-Checkup

Research: Type "Mental Health Checklist" into your search engine. Select "MHA Screening—Mental Health America." Through this, you will be made aware of various short, snapshot screenings for different types of common and treatable mental health conditions, and will be able to view the purpose of each category and complete a test/assessment for each.

Personally, I believe mental health is critical to overall wellness. In the space below, you may want to note your scores or thoughts about the screenings you took.

_____

_____

_____

_____

_____

CHAPTER 3

Family Element

Now we have encountered physical and mental health concerns. Let us see how we can grip life through another element of health: family.

Family is being explored next because family members influence us. In this book, family refers to birth parents, adopted parents, siblings, aunts, uncles, cousins, godparents, grandparents, in-laws, and other friends we hold close and dear to our hearts. These are the persons who are expected to care for us and show kindness to us. Thus, having listened to a few victims of abuse and child advocates talk about various types of abuse that children had reported on family members they thought they could trust, I believe that these negative experiences and circumstances, such as loss of loved ones, divorces, layoffs, and substance abuse, can cause one to have bottled-up anger that, if not treated, could cause mental issues.

Some children grow into adulthood with issues from family situations because they thought their living experiences and situations were normal family happenings. If adults are unable to cope with this type of past, they need to seek professional help from counselors, life coaches, or other mental health professionals so they can live a wholesome life, develop healthy relationships, and experience wholesome environments. Remember, what went on in house A may not have been the same practice in house B.

Having experienced a normal, healthy, wholesome, joyous family with an interactive, protected life, it was not until I was thirtysomething and employed as an elementary school principal that I encountered counselors' reports, Department of Human Resource visitors, and Child Advocacy Assemblies. I learned and went by established guidelines to report various types of child abusers to the appropriate authorities, becoming aware that crimes occurred involving mistreatment of children. These sessions were shockers to me. Imagine how the victims must have felt. Thus, I encourage children to report others who victimize them to counselors, teachers, principals, pastors, and other adults, including police officers, to get help. Also, keep in contact with relatives who have developed a wholesome relationship with you and who have shown that they care for your well-being.

Biblical Family Thought

And ye fathers, provoke not your children to wrath,
but bring them up in the nurture and admonition
of the Lord. (Ephesians 6:4 KJV)

Comment

In general, this means men should not purposely anger children
with unrighteous actions but nurture them.

Your Family Thought Reflection

Make comments below about your interaction with and reactions
to the family unit that you grew up in.

_____

_____

_____

_____

_____

CHAPTER 4

Vocational Health Element

Vocation, comprehensively defined, is a calling, profession, and trade that one has skills, qualifications, degrees, and certifications for that enable readiness for long-term employment. To add to this definition, I suggest that one needs to develop a legal, marketable job skill. This grows out of my observation that over the span of life, many factors can cause life to be unscheduled, unpredictable, and uncertain. Thus, the one you think may leave you an inheritance may outlive his or her money or other possessions.

At this point, you may think that you will marry into the fruit of your loved one's labor. What if your loved one changes his or her mind or gets a divorce? More than likely, his or her skills, degrees, and money will leave with that person. You may say, "the government will keep me up." Well, think about having a better quality of life than government-controlled handouts. Thus, if no one thrusts money on you through inheritance or marriage, you will indeed, need to work as a primary source of income, to help prepare for your future. In other words, at this point, your own skills may determine your salary, savings, and retirement or care, if you become disabled. Therefore, you may need to think about what type of job you qualify for or can be trained to do.

Other factors, besides qualifications for employment, that you might want to consider are the answers to the following questions:

- Do I want to work indoors or outdoors?
- Do I like driving all day and long distances?
- Would I like to work behind a desk, complete paperwork, or use my computer savvy?
- Do I have reliable transportation?
- What are my two best job skills?
- Do I want to work a day shift or a night shift? Is my job of interest seasonal or year-round?
- How much do I need to make each month to fulfill my needs or desires?
- What benefits does this job offer? Are said benefits suitable for my needs?

These are a few questions to answer before you begin to read want ads in newspapers, to check help-wanted posters, to complete applications, and to keep interviewing appointments. As far back as I can remember, it was understood through generations that everyone would work a full-time job, whether male or female. The men in my family worked forty years, and the ladies averaged thirty-three.

Work. It may make you more independent.

Biblical Vocational Health Thought

Whatever you do, work hardily, as for the Lord and not for men. (Colossians 3:23 ESV)

Comment

This verse reminds us to take work seriously.

Vocational Health Activity

Think about your vocational goals for the next three years and use the space below to write them down. Create some if you do not have any.

_____

_____

_____

_____

_____

CHAPTER 5

Financial Health Element

Since to a large degree one's job may be the main source of income, one's salary could influence a one's financial health. In this situation, I strongly suggest a yearly household budget based on one's take-home income. Nevertheless, this section of the book is not designed for a complete "money makeover" or "get rich quick" idea. Hopefully it will motivate the reader to review his or her spending habits, checking and savings accounts, credit card debts, loan rates, future retirement plans, and social security.

For investments, I strongly recommend the reader seeks an appointment with a lawyer and/or financial advisor. Usually, they work together on wills, trusts, estate planning, and investments for their clients. However, for daily living, a household budget may include monthly payments of bills, such as utilities, mortgage, vehicle notes, health insurance, life insurance, taxes, recreational allowance, gas for traveling, and food. Remember that once created and agreed upon with your partner (if you have one), the budget needs to be monitored to keep expenditures on track without too much miscellaneous spending, even if such is from your savings.

Although money does not have legs, I have heard of it getting away from lottery winners, and they become broke again. For ordinary people like me, a budget is very helpful. It has caused me to form the habit of paying *bills* and myself first.

Biblical Financial Health Thought

If they obey and serve him, they will spend the rest of their days in prosperity, and their years in contentment. (Job 36:11 NIV)

Comment

Although the above is my favorite Bible verse related to money, computer research shows many Bible verses related to money matters, if you care to read other verses.

Financial Health Plan

Use this space to create or *improve* your own monthly budget.

_____

_____

_____

_____

_____

CHAPTER 6

Social Health Element

The social element of life, in this book, refers to those pieces of life that help to make one a human being. One's birth experience of having been born by a human, growing-up experiences from childhood to adulthood with humans, and interacting with relatives, friends, and associates, as well as one's individual and group behavioral encounters, make one a social being.

According to a May 1, 2018, article by South University's Counseling and Psychology Department, titled "Why Being Social Is Good for You," having a strong network of support and community bonds fosters emotional and physical health, regardless of age. Therefore, one can benefit from wholesome activities with others. These benefits could include less stress, improved self-esteem, learned culture, changed social class, organizational acceptance, and job placement. In other words, one does not need everybody to love one; one just needs the right contacts through socializing that might improve one's status.

These interactions help one to adjust to various groups, establish relationships, and maybe meet a partner and mentor to pattern his or her future behavior after. In the words of Sivana East, "For a society to be healthy, its environment should consist of people who are mentally and physically healthy." She further addressed the fact that being socially engaged can boost the immune system and help one to live longer. Thus, if one wants to be more sociable, one could introduce oneself to others, become an organization's volunteer, join a group, and be kind to others. These acts will show others that you care about their well-being while respecting their boundaries.

It has been my experience and observation that these acts can help one cultivate friendships across culture lines.

Biblical Social Health Thought

A joyful heart is good medicine, but a crushed spirit dries up the bones. (Proverbs 17:22 ESV)

The Lord God said, "It is not good that men should be alone. I will make him a helper fit for him" (Genesis 2:18 ESV)

Comment

A joyful heart could grow out of positive, wholesome social experiences.

Social Health Action

Analyze your social life. Think about ways you might improve your social health and list them below.

_____

_____

_____

_____

_____

CHAPTER 7

Spiritual Health Element

According to the *Journal of Medical Ethics and History of Medicine's* April 9, 2018 article "Explanatory Definition of the Concept of Spiritual Health: A Qualitative Study in Iran," content analysis and in-depth interviews with twenty-two spiritual health experts included in the article, spiritual health is viewed as the connection with self (personal), others (social), nature (environment), and God (transcendental).

It is my opinion that spiritual health can improve mental health, social health, physical health, family health, vocational health, and financial health because God is part of spiritual health and has the power to grant healing to all the other types of health. Therefore, I am a strong believer that spiritual health can have dominance over other types of health because if one is a Christian or believer in the Almighty, one's character and value system would include religion and righteous practices in everyday life as one interacts with self, others, nature, and God. Thus, I believe if one sees God as one's Father, one would have self-worth as child of the King and would forgive and help others in need unconditionally as well as respect the beauty of nature from the bottom of the sea to the top of the sky.

As a Christian, one becomes a DIVA: a divine, intervening, victorious angel to help lead others to be living examples for Christ. To be living examples of Christ, they can be blessings to others if they abide by Matthew 25:34–36. These verses tell us that to enter the kingdom, we need to feed the hungry, clothe the naked, visit the prisons, and take in strangers. In other words, allow COVID to mean "concentrate on victims in despair."

Share your harvest with others too. Use your cell phone to encourage a youth or check on an elderly person.

Biblical Spiritual Health Thought

You shall serve the Lord your God, and He will bless your bread and your water, and I will take sickness away from among you. (Exodus 23:25)

Comment

The above verse attests *to blessings* that God gives to those who serve him.

Spiritual Health Reflection

Take a moment to reflect on and write about your spiritual health.

_____

_____

_____

_____

_____

AFTERTHOUGHTS

- Grip life! Hold on to every phase of your life: physical, mental, family, vocational, financial, social, and spiritual. Hopefully, reading my writing about these seven precious elements of life has inspired and motivated you, the reader, to improve your life and make an impact on the neighborhood in which you dwell for years to come. After all, COVID could mean "concentrate on victims in despair" for communities, organizations, individuals, cities, states, and nations.

- As I stated before, life's temperatures are like seasons. Its temperatures register hot, warm, cool, and cold. Which temperature does your overall health register on? Read the below thoughts and find out.

  ➢ If one's health registers hot, that person is a successful survivor and moving forward in an extraordinary way in all seven of the health elements.

  ➢ However, if one's health is registering warm, that someone could just be grading himself or herself average in one or two of the seven categories of health elements, or warm in all seven. Thus, one could check on improving self for a better quality of life.

➢ Now cool takes one's health temperature on a downward curve, below average. That someone needs to check self through suggestions made in at least four of the health elements for improving self.

➢ Wow. What about registering cold? If one is registering cold in all categories, that someone is dead to self and others. However, if one is registering cold in five or six health elements, one needs to look at those categories and seek help from an appropriate professional to move upward on the health element chart because that person's health may have an impact on self, children, and other family members. That person needs to make it a priority to improve self before causing loved ones to worry. As a matter of fact, that person may need solicited or unsolicited help or a supportive family member or friend to execute professionals' suggestions and directions in these health element areas.

• It is my prayer that you will be blessed and bless someone else with my book as a gift.

GRIP LIFE

Self-Help * Inspirational * Motivational

These are the health elements experienced by many as they grip life.

Dr. Elizabeth W. Grubbs has experienced life in and out of the United States. She is a product of Tuskegee University, University of West Alabama, Wayne State University, University of Mexico, and Los Angeles Institute in Education, Counseling, and Supervision.

She has taught elementary children and college undergraduates, has evaluated teachers, has written and directed federal grant programs, has served on a college trustee board, has been a member of a city zoning board, has been an area promotional missionary education director, has been appointed national validator for Early Childhood Centers Accreditation, was voted Chapter Zeta of the Year, was appointed AME Church steward, has directed a Native

American program, has coordinated school system assessments, has been a member of the Boys and Girls Club board, and has held many other supervisory positions. She was also selected Woman of History by Julia Harris Women's Missionary Society.

Manufactured by Amazon.ca
Acheson, AB